I knew I loved you when
I was waiting for you,
before I even knew your name,
before I had ever seen your face.

I dreamed of you, little one.
My heart was saving a special place,
just for you.

I knew I loved you when
I saw the tiny lines on a test.
Surprise! Joy!
My heart skipped a beat.

"You are coming!" I whispered,
and I hugged my tummy tight,
as if you were already there.

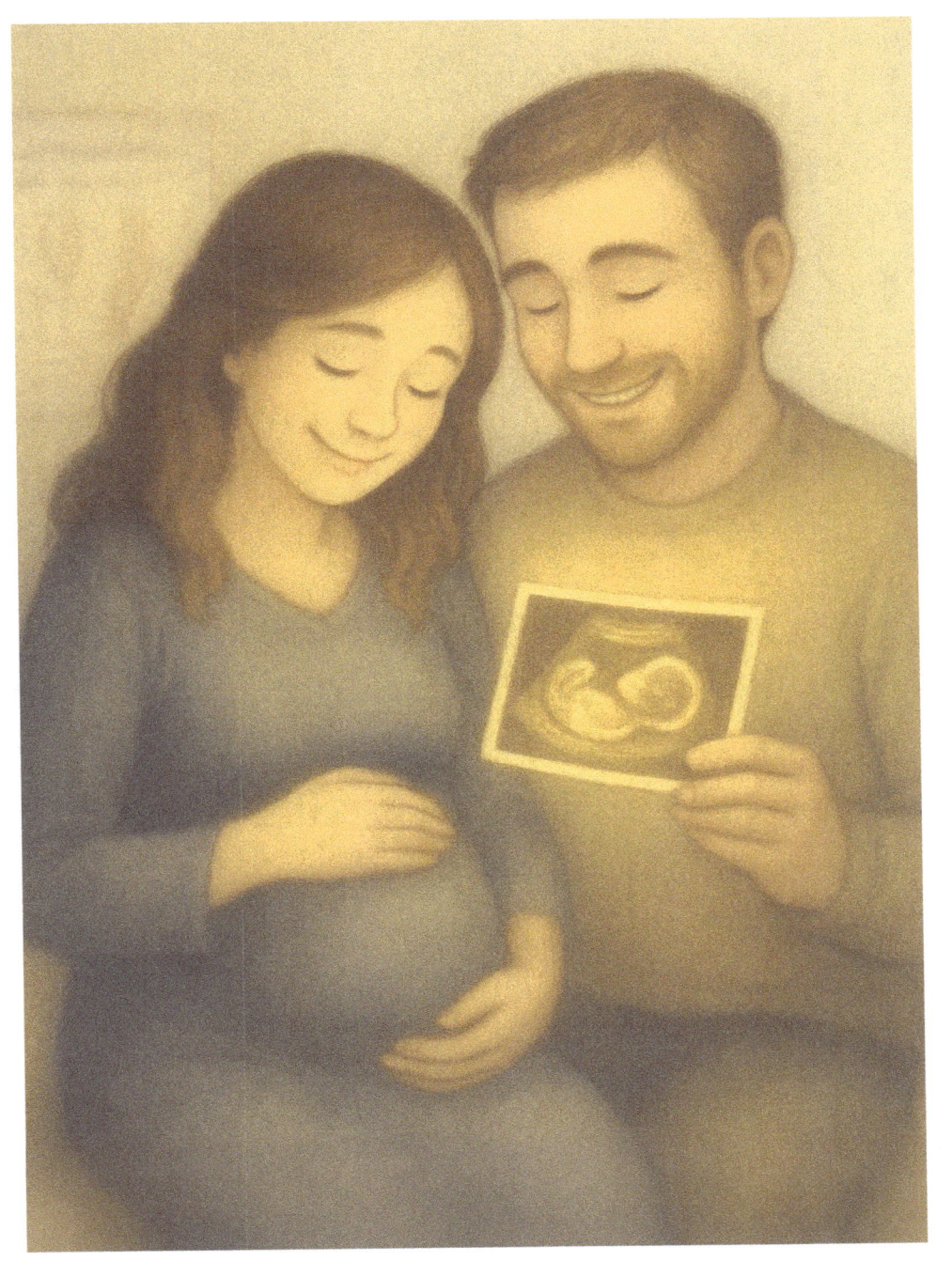

I knew I loved you
when I visited the doctor
and saw your picture for the
very first time—
a tiny bean, a tiny heartbeat,
strong and steady like a drum.

Every day, my love grew with
you. I was nervous,
but most of all, I was happy.

I knew I loved you
when I heard the words:
"It's a boy!"

My son. My sweet little boy.

I began to dream of your laughter,
your tiny hands,
the adventures we would
have together.

I knew I loved you when
I felt your very first kick.
Tap-tap, hello!

I sang to you, I talked to you,
and I wondered—
Would you like music?
Would you like stories?
Would you like the sound
of my voice?
Every flutter was a
a love note from you.

I knew I loved you when I worried.
Sometimes my tummy would tighten,
and I thought, "Is it time?"
But no—it was just practice.

Even in the waiting, even in
the worry,
my love wrapped around you
like a mama bear keeping her cub safe.

I knew I loved you when
the day finally came.
We rushed to the hospital,
waiting, breathing, hoping.
And then—
there you were.

Tiny fingers, tiny cries,
the biggest love I had ever known.
I looked at you and whispered,
"I knew I loved you when I saw you."

I knew I loved you when I carried you home.
We buckled you in,
we rocked you in our arms,
we showed you your very first home.

The house felt brighter,
the world felt sweeter,
because you were there.
I looked at you and whispered,
"I knew I loved you when I saw you."

I knew I loved you when
I had to leave you,
just for a little while.

I missed you every minute,
my heart counting the moments
until I could hold you again.

Love stretched like a string,
from me to you—
never broken, always strong.

I knew I loved you when I
first dreamed of you.
I knew I loved you when
I felt your kicks.
I knew I loved you when
I held you close.
I knew I loved you when
I missed you.

And today, tomorrow,
and every day after—
I will always, always love you.
Because my love grows with
my little boy,
forever and ever.